JUNGLE ANIMALS
ANIMALES DE LA SELVA

THIS EDITION
Produced for DK by WonderLab Group LLC
Jennifer Emmett, Erica Green, Kate Hale, *Founders*

Editor Grace Hill Smith, Libby Romero, Michaela Weglinski; **Photography Editors** Kelley Miller, Annette Kiesow, Nicole DiMella; **Managing Editor** Rachel Houghton; **Designers** Project Design Company; **Researcher** Michelle Harris; **Copy Editor** Lori Merritt; **Indexer** Connie Binder; **Proofreader** Larry Shea; **Spanish Translation** Isabel C. Mendoza; **Proofreader of the Spanish text** Carmen Orozco; **Series Reading Specialist** Dr. Jennifer Albro; **Curriculum Specialist** Elaine Larson

First American Edition, 2023
Published in the United States by DK Publishing, a division of Penguin Random House LLC
1745 Broadway, 20th Floor, New York, NY 10019

Copyright © 2025 Dorling Kindersley Limited
25 26 27 10 9 8 7 6 5 4 3 2 1
001-345924-August/2025

All rights reserved.
Without limiting the rights under the copyright reserved above, no part of this publication may be reproduced, stored in or introduced into a retrieval system, or transmitted, in any form, or by any means (electronic, mechanical, photocopying, recording, or otherwise), without the prior written permission of the copyright owner. Published in Great Britain by Dorling Kindersley Limited

A catalog record for this book is available from the Library of Congress.
HC ISBN: 978-0-5939-6661-7
PB ISBN: 978-0-5939-6660-0

DK books are available at special discounts when purchased in bulk for sales promotions, premiums, fund-raising, or educational use. For details, contact:
DK Publishing Special Markets, 1745 Broadway, 20th Floor, New York, NY 10019
SpecialSales@dk.com

Printed and bound in China
Super Readers Lexile® levels BR40L to 300L (English text)
Lexile® is the registered trademark of MetaMetrics, Inc. Copyright © 2024 MetaMetrics, Inc. All rights reserved.

The publisher would like to thank the following for their kind permission to reproduce their images:
a=above; c=center; b=below; l=left; r=right; t=top; b/g=background
Alamy Stock Photo: Glyn Thomas 16cb; **Dreamstime.com:** Aechevaphoto 4-5, Harry Collins 14-15, Dirk Ercken 17ca, 25ca, Andrey Gudkov 6-7, Pljvv 18-19, Roman Samokhin 3cb; **Getty Images:** Corbis / Fuse 27ca; **Getty Images / iStock:** Artush 8-9; **naturepl.com:** Eric Baccega 18ca, Anup Shah 12-13; **Shutterstock.com:** Dirk Ercken 24-25, 30bl, Lucas.Barros 11tl, Michail_Vorobyev 16-17

Cover images: *Front:* **Shutterstock.com:** ActiveLines, Stepan Kapl c, Nikolai Zaburdaev b;
Back: **Shutterstock.com:** Macrovector clb

www.dk.com

JUNGLE ANIMALS
ANIMALES DE LA SELVA

Camilla Gersh

Contents
Contenido

8	Parrots	
	Los loros	
10	Toucans	
	Los tucanes	
12	Orangutans	
	Los orangutanes	
14	Sloths	
	Los perezosos	
16	Sun Bears	
	Los osos malayos	
18	Gorillas	
	Los gorilas	

20	Giant Anteaters	
	Los osos hormigueros gigantes	
22	Tarantulas	
	Las tarántulas	
24	Poison Dart Frogs	
	Las ranas punta de flecha	
26	Tigers	
	Los tigres	
28	Jaguars	
	Los jaguares	
30	Glossary	
	Glosario	
31	Index	
	Índice	
32	Quiz	
	Prueba	

Enter the jungle, if you dare!
Look up!
Look down!
Look out!

Entra a la selva, ¡si te atreves!
¡Mira hacia arriba!
¡Mira hacia abajo!
¡Mira muy atento!

Parrots
Los loros

A parrot flies over the jungle. Its feathers flash red, yellow, and blue.

Un loro vuela sobre la selva. Sus plumas destellan rojo, amarillo y azul.

feathers
plumas

Toucans
Los tucanes

A toucan picks a berry with its large, yellow beak.

Un tucán toma una baya con su pico grande y amarillo.

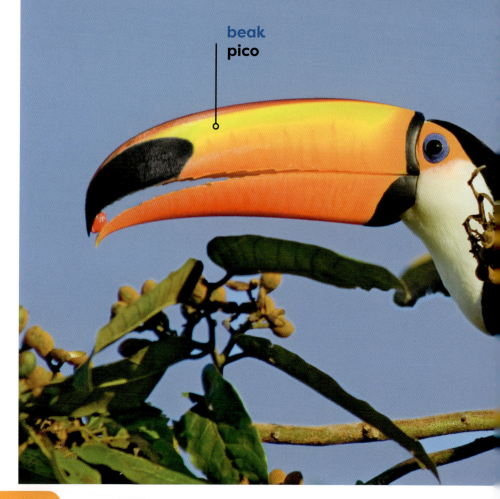

beak
pico

Orangutans
Los orangutanes

Orangutans swing from tree to tree.
They move very quickly.

Los orangutanes se balancean
de un árbol a otro.
Se mueven muy rápido.

Sloths
Los perezosos

Sloths live in trees.
They move very, very slowly.

Los perezosos viven
en los árboles.
Se mueven muy
muy despacio.

15

Sun Bears
Los osos malayos

Sun bears climb the trees. Their long claws grip the branches.

Los osos malayos trepan a los árboles.
Se sujetan a las ramas con sus largas garras.

claws
garras

Gorillas
Los gorilas

Gorillas live with their families.

Los gorilas viven en familia.

nest
nido

They make nests to sleep in at night.
Hacen nidos para dormir por la noche.

Giant Anteaters
Los osos hormigueros gigantes

An anteater sniffs an ants' nest with its long snout.

Un oso hormiguero olisquea un nido de hormigas con su largo hocico.

Tarantulas
Las tarántulas

A tarantula feels the ground shake with its hairy legs.

Con sus patas peludas, una tarántula siente un temblor en el suelo.

hairy leg
pata peluda

A tasty meal is moving nearby!
¡Una deliciosa comida se está moviendo muy cerca!

Poison Dart Frogs
Las ranas punta de flecha

A poison dart frog protects itself with its poison skin.

Una rana punta de flecha se protege con su piel venenosa.

25

Tigers
Los tigres

A tiger hides in the grass.
It watches and waits, ready to leap.

Un tigre se esconde en la hierba.
Observa y espera, listo para saltar.

Jaguars
Los jaguares

A jaguar rests. Shh!
Quiet in the jungle, please!

Un jaguar está descansando. ¡Shhh!
¡Silencio en la selva, por favor!

Glossary
Glosario

beak
pico
a hard, pointed bird's mouth
la boca dura y puntuda de las aves

claws
garras
sharp nails used to hold, climb, and grab
uñas afiladas que sirven para agarrar, trepar y atrapar

feathers
plumas
a soft covering on a bird's body
la cubierta suave del cuerpo de las aves

snout
hocico
a long, pointed nose and mouth used to smell and eat
parte larga y puntuda de un animal, donde están la boca y la nariz, que sirve para oler y comer

skin
piel
the outer layer of an animal, beneath fur and feathers
la capa externa de un animal, debajo del pelo o las plumas

Index
Índice

ants   20, 21

beak   10

branches   16

claws   16

climb   16

feathers   8

giant anteaters   20

gorillas   18

jaguars   28

nests   18, 19, 20, 21

orangutans   12

parrots   8

poison dart frogs   24

sloths   14

snout   20, 21

sun bears   16

swing   12

tarantulas   22

tigers   26

toucans   10

balancearse   12

garras   16

gorilas   18

hocico   20, 21

hormigas   20, 21

jaguares   28

loros   8

nidos   18, 19, 20, 21

orangutanes   12

osos hormigueros gigantes   20

osos malayos   16

perezosos   14

pico   10

plumas   8

ramas   16

ranas punta de flecha   24

tarántulas   22

tigres   26

trepar   16

tucanes   10

Quiz
Prueba

Answer the questions to see what you have learned. Check your answers with an adult.

1. Which jungle animal has red, yellow, and blue feathers?
2. Which jungle animal moves very, very slowly?
3. What does a giant anteater do with its long snout?
4. Which jungle animal has poison skin?
5. Name three other jungle animals. What do they do in the jungle?

1. A parrot 2. A sloth 3. It sniffs an ants' nest
4. A poison dart frog 5. Answers will vary

Responde las preguntas para saber cuánto aprendiste. Verifica tus respuestas con un adulto.

1. ¿Qué animal de la selva tiene plumas rojas, amarillas y azules?
2. ¿Qué animal de la selva se mueve muy muy despacio?
3. ¿Qué hace un oso hormiguero gigante con su largo hocico?
4. ¿Qué animal de la selva tiene la piel venenosa?
5. Nombra otros tres animales de la selva. ¿Qué hace cada uno en la selva?

1. El loro 2. El perezoso 3. Olisquea los nidos de las hormigas
4. La rana punta de flecha 5. Las respuestas pueden variar.